PRAISE FOR
THE PHOTOGRAPHER

The photographer in Ariel Goldberg's *The Photographer*—is a figure—is figuration—is both plural and singular, of pronouns, hearts, angles, sensual fields of urban minutiae and virtual fields of shifting reality, all that which is clamoring for photographic capture while remaining constitutionally resistant. It is a landscape strewn with lost and broken cameras that have gone viral beyond the human populations that proliferate, hoard and discard them while also searching, trying to save them and failing. Alas, Goldberg shows us just how deep we are into our most ecstatic roll around in the filth of representation, from which for nothing, no ethic, no sacred, no emergent, melodious song can we muster the oomph to tear ourselves away. —*Rachel Levitsky*

In this brilliant and inventive text, Goldberg presents photography not as an aesthetic pursuit, but an unavoidable task in the stream of daily chores; pictures must be taken, developed, printed, uploaded posted, shared, downloaded, analyzed, read, questioned, mistrusted, filed, stored, managed and deleted. The Photographer is engaging, funny, disturbing and profound. —*Zoe Leonard*

Ariel Goldberg's *The Photographer* is an astute and incisive meditation on the state of photography now. Quirky and playful, structured like a collection of snapshots, the tone is observational and upbeat. Nonetheless, *The Photographer* paints a devastatingly accurate portrait of a medium and technology that has reached its unholy apex of glut and saturation in the surveillance-subjected lives of digital makers and consumers. Goldberg seduces us with candid and intimate recordings of the quotidian, a world on the fly, but ultimately the picture drawn of the Internet revolution is chilling and dystopian. —*Moyra Davey*

THE PHOTOGRAPHER

THE PHOTOGRAPHER

Ariel Goldberg

ROOF BOOKS
NEW YORK

ISBN: 978-1-931824-60-6
Library of Congress Control Number: 2015933979

Cover photo, Ariel Goldberg, Newslip, 2013
Author photo, Ian Lewandowski, 2014

 This book is made possible, in part, by the New York State Council
on the Arts with the support of Governor Andrew Cuomo and
NYSCA the New York State Legislature.

Support also came from a 2012-13 grant from the Franklin Furnace Fund
supported by the Jerome Foundation; the Lambent Foundation Fund of Tides Foundation;
and by public funds from the New York City Department of Cultural Affairs
in partnership with the City Council.

Roof Books
are published by
Segue Foundation
300 Bowery, New York, NY 10012
seguefoundation.com

Roof Books
are distributed by
Small Press Distribution
1341 Seventh Street
Berkeley, CA. 94710-1403
800-869-7553 or spdbooks.org

You're the
photographer.

They didn't know I
was taking a picture.

No one was
commenting on my
photo then I realized
I posted it so only
I could see it.

No, you're the
photographer.

You want to take the
picture that is inside
your head and put it
inside someone
else's.

The images are
becoming more
disturbing as I see
them repeat.

It is hard to protect
a piece of electronic
equipment when
rocks and rubber
bullets are flying.

I put my nose up to a
photo that had an
eroded surface.

When I roll over the
picture, it becomes a
shade darker.

Am I blocking your
picture?

Which ones were
good or not proved
to be almost arbitrary.

I read by looking
at the pictures.

I don't have time
to take a good
picture anymore.

I don't want them to
like it or control it—
I want their guts.

Do you think they
are going to want
something explicitly
queer in the
photographs?

Is that a real photo?

Sometimes I think
it's easier for
war photographers
to take good pictures.

People were lining
up to take pictures
of me.

She barks at
the dogs she
photographs.

Just because
the moment feels
extraordinary
doesn't mean the
photo will be.

A better
photographer is
built in.

The slideshow
flashed a new photo
every eye blink.

I can't remember
the pictures I am
trying to remember.

They couldn't shake
my hand because
they were holding a
camera.

Can we go on a date
without your
camera?

If you have been
focusing on an
image now let it
fade.

Dear Photographer:

We put newspapers all over the perimeter of the room and taped them to the edge of the wall. It formed a very thin source of protection for the floor. I had to be careful with my feet not to step on a photo. I couldn't read the articles from that height, so those were fine to step on. I imagined the paint seeping right through when it dripped down. I tried to remember if I had seen the pictures before, or if they were new. I bent down to get up close to one picture. Maybe it was something I thought was relevant.

Dear Photographer:

The other day I began to find myself as I was online. I don't like the pictures of me, I complained. You laughed, as if welcoming me to the human condition. I guess I put them there at one point. I wish there were more people online who are obviously not me, you replied, with a generic name to be un-findable inside. What does that even mean. How does that company work that claims to control or improve your image? Apparently all they can do is write cease and desist letters to the websites that have an image of you. It's no guarantee the image will go away.

Dear Photographer:

I ordered a movie based on the keyword photography. Instead of watching it, I read and reread the courier font synopsis on the DVD jacket with names of characters and actors. Something like: A psychological thriller about a mentally unbalanced photo development clerk who becomes obsessed with a picture-perfect suburban family and gets involved when the façade starts to crumble. It was made nine years ago. Rated R. I sealed it. Carried it in my bag and mailed it back without watching it.

Dear Photographer:

We were standing around trying to make conversation but you seemed detached. Like you were listening and decided what we were saying wasn't interesting. You pulled a camera out of your tote bag and pointed it at the old map of the city that was hanging on the red wall above the stove. The sensor lingered as a blue spotlight for a moment over one of the rectangular folds.

I could not control
the backdrop.

Your camera kind of
looks like you.

You could pretend to
take pictures.

I denied the
photograph.

The journalists had
a shield of cameras.

Please tip when you
take a picture.

I have bags filled
with old negatives,
if you want them.

Can you send me some
nude pics?

The operator said
they'd talk to me in
between pictures of
my brain.

Is that it—that's it—
right there.

She is holding
the camera out
as far as her arm
can reach and
leaning back to
increase the space.

It's actually not a
peace sign, it's a pose.

Are you still taking
pictures?

I owe you a picture.

A low quality warning
appeared.

We're looking
for the person
responsible
for this picture.

Dear Photographer:

In the occult section, you found a paperback book on palm reading that features a famous photographer's hands. They were wrinkly and full of flesh, matching the figurative texture of a mountains' geography. It seemed absurd his hands were magical just because they had been the hands that held cameras that took good pictures. For skill to be in the hands sounds so random, so unintellectual. I wondered if the author knew the photographer or got the rights for the image's reproduction.

Dear Photographer:

I was reading about the photojournalist who just got killed and how he, at one point, took one of the most widely distributed photos to represent this war. A feature on the twelve-year-old girl in that photo was an adjacent story to his obituary. The article began with the subject looking at the photograph of herself from six years ago that she had never seen before. She put her hands over her face as she looked at the laptop. The photo was of her crouching, splattered in blood, watching her parents get shot to death. They didn't print the picture out for her.

Dear Photographer:

My housemate works for a digital photo-booth service that people rent for parties. He transports the camera in a rental car on the weekends. He also does Improvisational Theater as therapy. When he goes surfing the photo booth sits in our garage. I stared at the booth for brief intervals. I tried to understand how it was screwed together. The booth seemed as frail as a kid's science experiment with an aspect ratio gone wrong. Its shape resembled a porta-potty. Once I talked about the booth with him, how I'd like to get a picture in it, as if loading up on free samples at the supermarket. He said I'd have to come to one of the parties. But I wouldn't crash a wedding just for this photo booth. I wanted him to turn it on in the garage.

Dear Photographer:

I was at the recycling bin with my damp newspapers neatly bunched in twine. I saved them for the hope that time accrued would deliver purpose. Perhaps it was a misunderstood collection. I would counter doubts of letting go with reminding myself of realities like mold. An assistant photographed me holding newspapers above the bin in a ritualized farewell. Efficiency was reducing any memorializing. I was safeguarded from talking to the front-page photo and therefore protected from the photo talking back to me. Each paper I held became like a medal I had just won. The sun was harsh, so the shadows were too, and the garbage bins were ugly, or they were just recognizable to those who lived in this city.

People were
crowding around
your camera.

There's an American
flag in the back-
ground, is that ok?

Isn't a photo the
most complex and
compelling form of
identification?

The screen has no
backside.

I can express my
creativity through
photography without
difficulties.

There was a glare on
the photo album
pages.

The billboard read
picture perfect
deposits.

Lesbian Images is not
a picture book.

I don't know how
I will react to the
photos.

The file
self-destructs
in a few seconds.

Don't ask to see it
in focus.

We don't know
which photographer
took which picture.

They alert you if a
screenshot has been
taken.

Today you have to
take a picture.

The photographers
wait on the steps
fighting for the best
picture.

The photo turned
into a gift.

Too much is
combining.

I thought you took it.

It's hard to see.

I didn't want to get
caught taking the
picture.

Do you want me to
take your picture?

I disappeared to
take a picture.

The photos revealed
the hoax.

No—I disappeared
after taking
the picture.

I have that picture but
the other way around.

Dear Photographer:

As soon as they announced the cake, you grabbed your camera. I asked if you wanted me to be the photographer. You handed me the camera like it was a baton and rushed to the kitchen. I was in a relay race but standing still. I got stuck and couldn't see past the hallway crammed with people. The bookshelves made everything narrower. Someone sensed that I was trapped out of view and asked, "Where's the photographer?" It was at that moment I felt I had a purpose. I got pushed up to the entrance like I was about to win an award. But the first thing I saw was another person holding a camera and shooting. It's not a duplicate; they need their own version. I noticed it was a photo cake. The light in the room was terrible. Most shots came out in a blur instead of sharp edges for the faces. And the delay of the camera made me feel like I missed every shot I was intending. I held the camera out to you afterwards, sort of limp, "What do you want me to do with this?" In a gracious hostess voice you said, "Oh I'll take it," like the camera was a plate of finished food or an empty wine glass.

Dear Photographer:

Police say the mass shooting suspect dropped off a roll of film at the local photo development store with pictures of himself in a red G-string brandishing the weapon he used.

Dear Photographer:

The internet connection wasn't speaking to my computer. I began a familiar practice of clicking compulsively on the rainbow spread of bars. I was fully content passing the time like this, as if pressing an elevator button in private. No one else had to endure my pointless spout of anxiety. Then I noticed something I had never seen before. I was in that new browser that combines the search field with the address field. All the thumbnails of websites I had recently visited became rows of broken cameras. This default is an illustration in grayscale of a simple point and shoot with a raised flash opposite the shutter button. The break is literal: a zigzag through the lens. The exact middle of the camera was a fault line of cartoon lightning. The camera as weather report icon: half on stable land, half barely hanging on. I wanted to rip the broken half off, for the camera's loose tooth to be this tender upside down gap in the mouth, hot and metallic.

Dear Photographer:

I saw photos hanging on the walls in a museum and I was actually moved by them. It reminded me that photos could be good in a simple way. The photographer was someone who worked the graveyard shift in a big iconic building. Or maybe they just worked overtime consistently. They were grayish black and white 8x10s that made office life dark and weird. Wire tangles, arms hanging over cubicles, mirrors making that infinity field. It was genuine, which made me think about why I expect photos not to impress me.

THE NEWS

Publications get destroyed or reissued with the face blocked out.

I forgot about the way you hug.

A mega sized bouncy-ball of an eyesocket sits on the desk.

Emails return in a different font.

The tree swallows a chain like a mouth full of food tries to smile.

A temporary tattoo of a thong string is stuck for days.

Let's see if it comes out.

Antennae tilt and drip, sucking on gravity.

They now have neutral footage.

Scrubbing goes on and on then it ends.

The leaf just won't flush.

Drawers of old pens turn into judgmental storage loops.

She likes sprouts because they are like pubes.

The conversation piece falls off the table.

I am looking at something upside down to see if it has anything inside of it.

A melon scooped of its seeds.

The person I photographed weeks ago walks by me again on the street.

A nightmare of vitrine after vitrine.

The head of a fork faces the metal grates as if ready to eat them.

Hickeys wonder if they are just birthmarks.

The mirror image had a zoom lens.

A wind chime leans on a book with no paragraphs.

How do I answer the question about no lesbians being on TV?

What can be a resistant palette?

The soft pack sticks to the bathtub ledge like a gooey slingshot hand.

                                        The password is too gross to forget.

Bags slouch and lose their structure.

                    Flowerpots let go of extra water and it determines the pavement.

The smell of the sponge is on my hands and I still fall asleep.

                                A flash used to be a hazardous explosion.

I'm staring at sentences built on double negatives.

If you dig deeper in the bag you will find a less salty pretzel.

People are approaching killer waves with their cameras.

I bring this with me everywhere and panic at the thought of losing it.

When will wrinkled clothes be in?

I go to the bathroom during the short meditation and flush the toilet lightly.

The fish tanks are styled to look like screens.

                                    The next on line self-operates.

I copied something down I didn't mean to copy.

                              I sniff a communal eye pillow to see how it holds on to decay.

There is news of a photographer no one knew about being a great photographer.

                                    People shush the ones who clap too soon.

Last time I misread soft pack as stopwatch.

Tiny spikes outdo the sign.

Headlines refresh before I get to the old ones.

Chaos approaches to cross its eyes on the copyright.

A screen is getting more sensitive.

The person I stole my haircut from is here—no—it's someone else with that haircut.

A digital camera is now featured on the mural.

Auto share is built in.

A wire gets pulled from a clump of wires with suspense.

I cannot tell which one is the smaller or bigger boob.

The bald spot finds replacements in the blind spot.

I collect how people do air quotes differently.

You can clip a camera to your neck that takes pictures for you.

I handed the cashier an old receipt with the money.

A thought relies on the list as a version of oxygen.

Not a blind carbon copy.

Dollar stores and car services face each other playing the same radio station.

Can you minimize your presence?

The deli next to the deli has a real personality.

Kids laugh at the drag performer on the subway platform.

Disinfectant wipes poke from the dispenser in a stout ponytail.

Instead of fixing the ornate doorknob they drilled a generic one directly above it.

The guy on a laptop in the corner is an orbiting satellite.

The sign reads big sale.

Used gum in an empty water bottle is a display-case for the brain.

My right click is broken.

The rocks on the beach are an all right gift shop.

The hand dryer blows extra air on the garbage bag.

It's really important to know your category.

You can drop it smash it crack it anywhere in the world.

PRESS CONFERENCE

Inside an old factory turned art space sits an audience of 25 people in folding chairs. There is no air conditioning. They share the experience of sweating while watching the performance. The Photographer and Assistants demount three stacks of newspapers. The audience rotates their chairs to follow them towards the opposite wall. One Assistant tilts a cluster of microphones towards The Photographer. The microphones trail as a mane of unplugged cords. There is one working microphone in the mix. The Photographer approaches a cement podium and stands on an incomplete set of books entitled The Encyclopedia of Photography *to increase their height. The other Assistant operates a monitor hooked up to a free download of a teleprompter application on a laptop. The Photographer's text begins to scroll.*

Good Evening. I stand before you to address a certain fading aura around our cameras. Let us conflate the positions of subject, photographer, viewer as the tasks of asking for and receiving permission tumble into a default of radio silence. Perhaps someone out there utilizes a loosely adhered post-it note reminder, but we will not see permission built in as a button on future models. This disappearance of permission represents a robust threshold for our supposedly magical medium.

Imagine you are buckled into a rollercoaster ride. A camera is programmed to get you right in the middle of the drop. At this precise moment, you cannot take that picture. You cannot be on the ground to even arrange that picture. As you shuffle out of the ride and search through a grid for your face you notice the picture is a little more than overpriced. The permission is wrapped up in a reverse order. Perhaps the camera got you screaming with your eyes closed. If you say no thanks to the souvenir, the data slips away as another seizure beyond our grasp in the consortium of photographic records.

Outside amusement parks, our vows to permission fluctuate daily along a spectrum of volatile denial to harmonious indifference. The staff photographer is barely there. The unknown photographer is not unrelated to the cameras strapped on like choker necklaces to streetlights. The person as presser of a button of an informative image in most cases becomes anonymous. The name of the website where the image of "the revolution" was posted comes to stand in the place of where the photographer's name used to be.

You might feel compelled to contribute to the maelstrom your own shot of the tour bus landlocked by protestors. You notice the blurry photo you had taken is already there, posted. You are then reminded of that moment when it seemed people were not only marching together, but were taking pictures together. And they were marching because of what many sets of images have exposed. The crises of our times are so urgent they produce confusing foreclosures of permission. Of course, this line of inquiry depends entirely on who holds the camera and where it is pointed.

The general public now feeds multiple systems for consuming images that have blossomed as platforms for advertisers to infiltrate. These systems have even automated such basic maneuvers as the identification of ourselves if we appear in a photo. Meanwhile the classic techniques, such as shooting from the hip, take extensive trial and error training in a human's connection to their gadgetry. To circumvent permission is a real skill for real photographers. The street photographer of last century, in their mythical heyday, would not stop to ruin their future photos with a polite interruption. Or just imagine the wildlife photographer, who counts among their equipment a cage to be safeguarded inside during quiet lapses from opportune moments.

Which leads me to wonder: have you ever been chased for photographing a display of raincoats in a market that had no permit to be selling their goods? Have you ever blocked the lens of the camera that might aid the government in identifying dissidents?

Perhaps to answer these questions you could visit a museum that is holding an exhibition designed to assess the pulse of photography. In the farthest room of the downstairs gallery, you could watch documentation of a performance lecture about videos, found online, from a warzone. The question is how we, who are not there, translate "seeing" the military killing people who are resisting this country's government. A person holding a camera on the balcony of their apartment building gets shot and killed by a sniper within their own video. On the opposite wall to the performance lecture are stills cataloguing several instances of death while photographing. They are blown up on glossy paper beyond the intended resolution. The photos are both attached to the wall and weighed down with informal binder clips. They are not framed.

Consider how a "No Cameras" sign usually accompanies art that is classified by preservationists as old or falling apart in a museum amidst climate control machines sitting like hedgehog figurines that hold a key in their belly for someone to enter your home who ordinarily wouldn't have a key.

People bring cameras inside museums. The coat check doesn't want them. They don't want to be responsible for your bag falling from a cubby and an irreversible dent occurring. Or the intolerable beeping of a camera after it wakes up from a nap. Museums are becoming even more accommodating to people and their cameras. Comments in one suggestion box unanimously read, "I would rather take my own pictures than buy the art selected for reproduction on a postcard or a book in your gift shop." In some museums, you can simply pay a fee to be allowed to take as many pictures as you like.

Photography has become akin to a light lawlessness in a museum. It's like the power you might feel when jaywalking. I have watched guards, who are just doing their jobs, reprimand photographers who go too far, who claim not to know how to turn off the flash on their cameras. I don't blame people for crossing this marked boundary; I don't know if they can help it.

Which brings me to the acquisition of automatic behavior. Those producing children within a culture where cameras flow rapidly are in the routine of photographing their children when they are first born and growing up. It seems the same is true for proud pet owners.

A parent probably does not ask their baby if they can take their picture. Or if they do, they cannot expect a response. Imagine a child's first words being: "go ahead and take my picture!" Perhaps deep in your unconscious lives your very first interaction with photography as a moment when you were a subject who did not (because you could not) give permission. The routine stands in for a deceptively satisfying exchange. I once heard a three year old sing with excitement, "show me me" when she wanted to have her picture taken, and taken again.

Toy cameras are rugged enough to be dropped or thrown. Yet children inevitably tire of the toy camera. It is possible to chart, like their growth in height, how the child becomes a teenager by learning the rebellion of looking unhappy or inaccessible inside a posed photograph.

As agency oozes into one's life so does the illusion of control, at least via the profile, for the subject to just be the photographer. This is one clue as to why permission is fading from the vernacular: we would just be talking to ourselves.

Photography has become enthroned in the mirage of an inextinguishable resource. The memory cards of the world are being discarded as I speak and replaced with newer ones to fit inside newer cameras to hold more pictures. Memory cards enter the waft of toxicity to be foraged, reconstituted and resold. But these materials are not simply ether even if the pictures stored on them become too many to keep, too many to know.

In other words, what do we give ourselves permission to look at when treading water as neither photographer nor subject? This is more a question of how much time in a day we have to look. Or how healthy will it be for us to search for photographs of the person who broke our hearts? When scrolling through a grid of pictures named, "the sunset," how do we manage the fraught inception of these images? I hear an echo of this question from many a leading philosopher on photography, alive or dead.

Which leads me to the reverberation of the first time I saw a color photo on the cover of the newspaper. It was like staring at a fantastic photograph—the looking at just the change. And this moment of, "wow" got replaced with the first time I saw mostly color photos. And then this experience got replaced by seeing less important photos appear in black and white. This experience continues to get replaced.

I am losing myself! Let us return to a fairly modest scenario of asking for permission. Imagine you locate a desire to photograph two women with matching red dyed hair and matching earrings riding the bus with just one windbreaker intimately draped over both their shoulders. You are sitting behind them and decide on this angle. You turn off the sound of the camera shutter to be more covert. Meanwhile, you remain haunted by the fact that the photo would be much better if you took it with your face to their faces. Our lives seem smoother if we excise the conversation of asking for permission.

Perhaps this desire for a photo of intriguing strangers does not seem like the wars being operated from drones that rely on photo-based technology. But you still feel those drones' electromagnetic fields when tapping with your finger grease the flat screen that signifies a shutter. Serendipitously, you are reminded that your data is all filled up. With this reminder comes the sinking feeling of all the other photographs happening at this moment. You may feel a total breakdown in action, unable to deal with the decisions necessary to make more space on your camera-phone.

Where are we? Permission, or the infinite breach of it, translates to the elastic walls of whatever room we are in. Come in to my home, look at my bat-mitzvah album is very different than log in and stare at the pictures of the party you weren't invited to. Your RSVP to the wedding, by the way, signs off your permission to be photographed at the wedding. Wedding photography is one of the last stable and lucrative industries for "the professionals."

Forget weddings! Even if you are at a party, you are a real wet blanket if you prefer not to be photographed. I cannot remember the last time I saw a person refuse to be photographed among friends. Actually, I do remember. It was at a poetry reading! It was a person reading poetry in a bookstore and she said, "No—stop! I don't want my picture taken," as soon as the photographer lifted the camera over his face.

And no wonder that photographer didn't "ask first." Once I watched these people photograph their friend's ass crack at that bar Cubbyhole while she sat drunk and distracted. When the friend was presented with the cell phone photo of her ass crack, she just laughed.

Meanwhile, I have never felt more affection towards a friend than the one who tried to intervene with a photographer in the front row of a crowd at a sweaty lesbian dance party with a stripper theme in a hip yoga studio slash healing space. The photographer didn't appear to know anyone they were photographing. My friend reported back to me: "Some people here are exhibitionists; they might have said yes if he just asked." I think the photographer thought he was swallowed whole by the exponentially growing psychic pictures around him and emerged invisible.

You might at this point be considering the sex-text. There have been more than several cases where a teenager initiates a naked photograph to a love interest and then the person who sent or received the photo lets it go viral and the subject is tormented and the localities are befuddled with various possibilities of prosecution.

And so, how different is our routine of taking pictures of people who may not identify as one of the wonders of the world than taking a photograph of one of the wonders? The concept of the still life is expanding on to the living. We must consider that even if we are not tourists, we are historically forced to watch them.

What does the law have to say about our dying language of permission? You might remember how the president attempted to control, and this I must note was a pathetic attempt, the official photos of a recently killed enemy.

The news story was about deciding not to release "the photos." They were classified.

What we did see was a picture of politicians and their advisors at a decision-making table looking at the photographs the military took. It is my theory that the gory photo of the killed enemy we can still see fake or leaked versions of would have looked too much like the gory images that the troops are taking. However much the military may try to produce a positive image of their operations, with embeds and the electronic fence around them, we will see an undertow of horrific images. The illogical routines of our wars bank on the concept of reckless permission. If a self-determined political power decides they can occupy another country, this pretext allows for images to exceed permission.

The representatives who speak at press conferences, not unlike this one, to clean up the messes of horrific photos, note they don't permit the photos—as if someone could, and would. The lack of permission enables life-altering photos to spread. It is not only the photographer who is eerily not asking permission, but the hungry public.

One always has the option of giving up on being the photographer. Perhaps this is all I am here to say to you tonight. I welcome you to the future of this medium through its catalogue of malfunctions.

Thank you, and goodnight.

MORE NEWS

A fountain is on in the rain.

We are testing you to spell out the acronym.

I cut the cut off shorts too short.

A photographer shot in the eye with a rubber bullet will probably lose his vision.

Who is they?

I thought the cicadas were a fire alarm.

The photo makes someone a hero.

I shout the word representative in the automatic answering system.

The baked goods wrapped in plastic get dusted regularly.

Phlegm is stuck on the drain's net and limps before an escape.

For a glass window to not reflect, I lean my torso separate from my legs.

The street should not look so much like the street.

It doesn't look good enough, at first, or it looks all-wrong.

Miniature butterfly clips hold up orchid stems.

Your whole body can be a napkin.

Knuckles crack, as a thought.

Stiff legs slow down the whole street's movement.

I don't want to have a bath in your bath water.

I'm so sick of this historical moment.

A mouth is joined with envelope breath.

How do you make this visible?

They're blowing on a lens like they're going to kiss it.

The vanishing point of an unzipped fly.

I can't tell if it's dead or just dormant.

I keep taking these pictures that are almost good, but not good enough.

Are you into anything radical?

Changes are now known as shocks.

We could eliminate the non-useful ambiguities.

Arrows get painted on during the presentation.

It's possible I've outgrown my inquiry.

Confusion is an infinite field of time.

I would not get a buzzword tattooed on my ass.

A scarf drags on the floor then dirt wraps the neck unnoticed.

We want to be outside these conversations.

I get wall-eyed.

Here the revolution was treated as an institution.

We have to be careful not to become nostalgic.

I liked it but for the wrong reason.

When the radio station closes just one song plays on repeat.

Why don't you get the gender-neutral bathroom app?

That tote bag goes nicely around the neck.

Half half price.

The stick shift is made from a plunger and a vibrator.

I entered the bathroom like it was a darkroom.

That was not fact checked.

Let's photo bomb it.

That was almost professional.

The clocks are off from each other like a family with nothing in common.

They patented taking a photo against a white background.

A sign needs the backbone of a cane.

Uniformed officers will soon be wearing cameras during every shift.

I'm glad you're zooming in on this.

Someone sprinkled dog shit with glitter one clump after another.

You can delete the ones of yourself later.

I crossed it off my list because I didn't want to do it.

You can buy the domain dot photographer.

At the end of the day the revolving door gets flattened down the middle.

A few thousand followers is nothing.

Elastic spouts for the hands silence the shutter.

Do you recognize this—how do you recognize this?

You need a photo on the cover if you want people to pick up the book.

I swallow an eyeball with the point of my tongue against my cheek.

Data was scooped up.

A dismembered toilet is camera ready.

The skeleton mannequin tilts over when wheeled across the room.

I'm not high-fiving that.

The legend may be disappointing.

My image is just floating around.

The original form is held hostage for a daily rate.

The double S in the word Newsstand looks wrong.

Sidewalks are only on one side of the street.

I see a lot of people with their eyes closed.

Dear Photographer:

I have now heard the story about the photographer getting a camera implanted surgically in the back of his head on the international and local news. The camera takes a picture every minute and is immediately uploaded to a museum installation on the other side of the world. This photographer has a publicist. He says the surgery was more painful than he expected. The private university where he works asked him to wear a lens cap. It's custom made, like a sleeping mask, to wear over the camera when he is on campus.

Dear Photographer:

I discovered a game called Photo Hunt at the bar. I peered over sets of shoulders to learn how it works. The idea is to find where two of the same soft porn photos don't match because of retouching mishaps. For example: you tap where a bikini strap is missing in one photo but is squeezing against the skin of the leg in the other. The area to hunt is often tussled, like a swirl of water moving opposite to the current. I had to guess if the photos were altered to not be replicas or if the game company buys real mess-up photos from the magazine.

Dear Photographer:

In a documentary about discovering you're a lesbian as a kid, the director includes interviews, dramatizations, and of course, black and white photos. Nothing matched up exactly: it was a collage of stories, premonitions and imagined experiences. When the credits rolled, childhood photos were listed as if a leading role in the film. The names of people who contributed photos were formatted as a block of text. There was no way to know who was responsible for providing what photo. Bullet points separated the names. The photos were this waft of collective purpose, self-effacing enough to be cohesive, something I imagine political movements strive for in gaining temporary momentum.

Dear Photographer:

The picture begins as a seamless diptych of overhead views, shot from a plane. You can switch between the photos by sliding along the bottom of the frame by holding down your mouse. The default is before the disaster and the sliding reveals the after. They work together in this way like a squeegee on a dirty window. The software simulates shuffling through a pile of photos in your hands.

A van drives by with
cameras twirling on
a rooftop tripod.

Soldiers played dead
for the camera.

Steadiness results in
sharpness.

I've had one picture
open for days.

Say cheese doodle.

You are not authorized
to see these pictures.

We don't stop what
we are doing
to recognize
the camera.

I'm experiencing a
loss of detail.

It was either a friend
or a stranger who
took it.

We are relying
on cuteness
to balance it out.

I did do some
unpeopled pictures.

You never know when
a good picture
is going to happen.

I saw the full moon
and then I saw
someone take a
picture of it.

Is posing for photos
a weakness?

I didn't want to
waste film on
another angle.

I've become such an
image whore.

No pic, no proof.

You must have
made this pixilated
on purpose.

Officers have no right
to see photographs or
delete them.

Life doesn't have to
stop for amazing
photos.

I took about a
thousand pictures.

I want to show you
how perfect it was.

We have the images in
our head already.

I blurred the faces be-
cause we didn't have
permission.

Hold on.

THE SALE

An audience fills most seats in the auditorium of an art school with bold architecture. The evening includes snacks, wine and a medley of 10-20 minute performances to support the beloved local literary non-profit. Four Assistants enter the stage. One Assistant rolls out a suitcase that would be indecipherable on the baggage claim if not for its heavily torn upholstery. The Photographer approaches a sleek podium in a leather jacket that exudes shoulder pads. They hold a travel coffee mug and ignore the Assistants, who begin to manage a bundle of objects from the suitcase in their arms. A low techno beat begins. The Assistants walk up and down the aisles of the auditorium while hoisting up featured photo-accessories. The Assistants are split in pairs to move like conveyer belts in the aisles: two begin at the top of the auditorium while the other two begin at the bottom of the stage. A puddle of dead stock remains on stage to be rotated in and out of their arms after each lap. They are stoic, sexy and graceful. The Photographer appears to have their speech memorized.

Welcome to my garage sale of accessories that keeps pictures flowing rapidly.

I'll begin with quoting an advertisement that I cut out from an old professional photography magazine. The tagline reads, "Tired of fumbling for film?" We see a close-up of the torso and jeans area, comfortably clothed. Attached to this person's belt is a leather pouch that holds three rolls of 35-mm film. This ad stands at a threshold: pre-cell phone, pre-beeper, but not pre-gun.

I'll go through my whole inventory for you tonight. My assistants are holding up various goods, to eventually fall in sync with my description.

Central to my collection is a "No Cameras" sign. I bought it off the internet in my sleep. In real life, you can find the "No Cameras" sign at the airport and the dentist. Perhaps you also want to create a place where photographs are not allowed? The sign recognizes the threat photography holds, just as the "Photo Enforced," warning near traffic lights hopes to induce punitive fear.

Moving on, I have these special envelopes from local one-hour photo places. They don't really call it one-hour any more. The pharmacies blast the word photo on the window, alongside words like, "drugs" and "beauty." Some facades bear the palimpsest of the words, "One-Hour" on the sign. I have an envelope that reads, "Improve your Image." Another, "Memories Matter!" Please note the exclamation point. I don't remember what pictures I got developed to get the envelopes. They probably weren't my pictures.

Speaking of what's laying around your home, I have here tonight the "double A" battery and its counterpart, the charger. These are transitional figures in the first wave of digital cameras. Early models employed the "double A" as if referencing something like a hammer. The miscellany from a hardware store could fuel the innovation. I once had three different hand-me down cameras that all used the "double A" battery. But these cameras could only survive a few pictures before the batteries went caput.

One day, you might find a camera on the beach. This happened to me. And after the initial luckiness wore off, I felt confused, like, did this wash up? Is it a message in a bottle or environmental activism gone wrong? The camera died shortly after I looked at all the photos already on it. Newlyweds or something. A baby shower. Work friends. I ordered a battery charger. Then I realized the battery was actually, totally dead. Was the camera simply left behind for this reason? It became too much of a hassle to bring back to life.

I have found myself saying that I would stop shopping for this photo detritus. Then I came across a magnificent fake camera, miniature, three-quarters the size of a real one but hollow and plastic. The last time I had a fake camera it was a squirt gun and a keychain. I lost it through the gaps of my shopping cart at a site-specific performance.

I'm much happier with this fake camera anyway. The flash is non-negotiably attached. Also, this one came with a Bratz sticker on the back that I tried to rip off then just came to accept. Most of the buttons don't depress. The lens is fixed, so you cannot turn it to pretend to be adjusting the f-stop. The backside doesn't open. But you can look through a plexi-glass viewfinder. Editing the world still works. The advance lever also works: it makes a clicking sound, faint. And the numbers under a little bubble increase, so you know when all the pictures you haven't really taken add up. Finally, it has a hand-strap to put around your wrist. You can wear it as a bracelet.

This brings me to accessorizing. I have two t-shirts with 35-millimeter film cameras on them. These shirts are supposed to look like you are wearing a camera around your neck. But the optical illusion only works from a distance. The signifier of "liking" photography that these shirts imply is outdated. Liking photography is now anachronistic because it is just so functional. I have worn these shirts often underneath other shirts. They have been valued gifts to me from loving people in my life.

One shirt's tag reads Grrrl Small. The other reads Lady, definitely a "baby-tee." They speak the truth: we can carry around a simulacrum of the camera as if it were a security blanket, or as flat as a printed photograph used to be. A t-shirt with a camera on it expresses effortlessly the camera's desire for weightlessness. This is different than a record player on a tote bag, I can assure you.

I also have here a box with an order form you can send to a company to put a photo (of your choice) on a plate. Literally: you can eat off your pictures.

This brings me to a question I always get asked, "Do you sift through boxes of old family photos at flea markets?" No. I would only be reminded of the burden that comes with my own kin's collective documents. I've seen my parents throw out whole albums when consolidating their belongings. They put some, but certainly not all duplicates of flowers pictured in bloom, inside these potentially archival shoeboxes. Periods of time become efficient storage.

And so, the majority of what I have to show you tonight are albums. There is a cache of photos that is mostly dormant, living inside my brain, and it communicates, yearns, for emptiness. I don't know if the album is like a cathartic landfill or a reminder of the landfills.

I've developed a complex relationship to the albums. If you have anxiety about photography, take my ritual as a functional script. I recommend meditating in front of all of these blank albums and a video camera for at least half an hour. I don't know how often. The more blank albums that surround you, the better. I would set them up on a couch to simulate being crowded in. Then spread them out. Really explore the textures. I posed them. I did this in the morning when the light was the most dramatic and my mind fresh from its trip to the subconscious.

I am not selling my albums all together as a lump sum like fine china or anything. You can split up the collection. I want to disown these accessories, eventually. I may just have to donate my collection back to the great archipelago of thrift-stores from whence it came.

Anyway, I would always empty the albums I collected or I would buy the ones that were old but new and never filled. The best ones have sat somewhere for years and light stained the space around where a photo was trapped. What results is a nice variety of shades that pan out, like abstract images of light leaks.

The best type of album you could get here tonight has corrosion on it from photographs that were deteriorating for whatever reason. You could buy hazardous material from me—really! One item in my collection that is not for sale is the classic *Overexposure: Health Hazards in Photography*, which is also available as a book on tape, somewhere, out there.

Who needs a photograph inside the album when you have traces of light and chemicals? I am pleased to announce the fundamental aspects of the photographic medium are strongly intact here tonight in this profusion of crap!

I wonder if I haven't
heard from you, it's
because of the photos.

The caption read
protestor, not your
name.

We pacified you by
taking a picture.

The size of the photo
was too big for the
screen.

I am so glad you are
not one of
those warzone
photographers.

You will see a photo,
but the photo will not
help you answer the
question.

How did the photo-
journalists arrive in
time?

I changed the
wallpaper.

I never get sick of
looking at these
pictures.

Why do we have to
look at pictures?

The witness says it
was all for the picture.

If you take a picture
of the building it
might look like you
are trying to destroy it.

I'm still working on
my images.

I meant to send it, not
post it.

You don't like it when
I take your photo.

We need to do a
group photo.

I couldn't find a
picture of you in the
database.

The radio still has no
pictures.

If they've chosen
a picture it will
appear, if they
haven't, a generic
shape of a head will
represent them.

There's been a
caption error.

I don't care; let them
take pictures.

Cannot record.

Why not post all the
readers' photos and
let the public vote?

A masked person
took a picture.

A question mark
appeared to indicate
the photo could not
be found.

Can the user see that
I've looked at their
photos?

Dear Photographer:

I walked by a street vendor who hangs his photos with thick packaging tape on scaffolding rods. The photos are matted and then stored in plastic sleeves. They are of street signs, landmarks, and the city in motion. The plastic sleeves attach to the sticky side of the tape and at the end of the day he rips these display images off. Rough and graceful.

Dear Photographer:

I offered to take the picture you needed of the clock tattoo on your arm. It's a hand drawn circle with a jumble of numbers in one asymmetrical side. You had to turn it unnaturally by holding your boob away from your arm. It has to be a picture you kept saying, not just a snapshot. With a composition you demanded. I know, I said. It was like we were siblings. We tried different backdrops: a table, bookshelf, decorative fabric. I hated that I was moving things around. Or I was disappointed that things would need to be moved around. You wanted to keep looking at what I took and then referencing this one that was almost okay but not good enough. The photo was for a show, to be on a wall. To take the pressure off you said it didn't have to get done now. These could be sketches, but I insisted we do a few more. Then you said let me see, stop, that's the best one. But I didn't understand how it was different.

Dear Photographer:

Your flash was tilted diagonally to the ceiling with a bounce card tucked behind it. You were turning towards the more interesting people, or the ones interested in each other. You paused in front of those who registered they would be solidified into versions of their movements. Then there were the ones who didn't notice you until the light of the flash got under their eyelids. If the dancing was deep, they appeared not to notice you at all.

Dear Photographer:

We were talking about how its funny that people change. This was in reference to being in a school portrait or sitting on Santa's lap. I thought I'd tell the story of being Santa's photographer at the mall. Our photo studio was set up in the entranceway to a bankrupt department store. This was a downgrade from winter wonderland's position in the center of the food court. The whole operation was living through a pay-cut. Customers would tell us about how the other Santa place had gone digital but they were staying loyal to us. They wanted the same Santa, so tracking the progress of people growing seemed more exact. I had to shake a toy to make babies smile, which didn't always work. Sometimes if the babies were crying I just took their picture anyway, figuring tears would be hard to detect if they hadn't accumulated enough to gloss their faces. Sometimes the parents refused to pay for the pictures I'd taken of their crying babies and I had to redo them. As punishment, I'd be switched to the register, which meant slipping the photo into a card or cutting it to fit into a keychain or a snow globe. I was always afraid of ruining the photo with these more intricate holders.

DELETE.

                                                    Are you, like,
                                                    anti-digital?

I didn't pose.

I had no choice but to
pose.

If I didn't pick up the
pictures by a
certain date they
would be thrown
away.

Copying is
frequently
the only method
for recovering
a deteriorating
photograph.

I have more memory
than I know what to
do with.

I'm going to follow
them with my camera.

Stop operating the
camera immediately if
it emits smoke.

I buried my camera
in the sand once I
realized it was
totally broken.

They feel very
threatened by your
pictures.

We responded to cues
like jump or fake
laugh.

Someone holds a
blown up picture in
the funeral
procession.

Location is an instant
category.

They took pictures of
us in a back room.

I found my photo
used without
permission.

Editing will happen
naturally with the
passage of time.

Let's do one
traditional and one
zany.

I love walking
through peoples'
pictures.

I am so sick of
photography.

The suspect and
victim each had
their own portrait
alongside the story.

I want my subjects
not to care.

I scrolled over the
grid of pictures as if
looking for a face in
a crowd.

The back of the
photo looks kind of
erotic.

The camera was my
only audience.

Dear Photographer:

I searched nearby, which was a button. I found the pharmacy then dragged the mouse over the store's awning so I could see if they had processing. They did. I walked through the nearby streets up to the self-service station with a flash-drive in my pocket. I had no intersections to wait at. I arrived at the screen and proceeded through options like prints, calendars, and photos on objects. They even make crystalline trinkets. As soon as I began my selections, a programmed voice also gave instructions. I looked for a button to turn off the voice. The screen next to me was also activated; someone began their order a few minutes before mine and the machines were talking to both of us at once. I enjoyed the predictions. The echo mixed with the classical music in the air of the store. I lost my place on the screen for size and quantity. I was putting my ear up to the speakers. I had to start over. How did I end up with border options like balloons or a jungle? I went to the register with a receipt before I could get my photos. It was like cashing in at an arcade while checking in at an airport. I returned to the machine to scan the barcode. Slowly but quickly, a spout delivered my prints. They landed on each other. I thought they would need time to dry before getting stacked.

Dear Photographer:

You jumped up from the table, reminded, to show us the picture. It was printed out from the album section of a profile page onto regular office paper, which gave the backside a dark cloud of opacity. The page felt wet. The picture was mostly of a baby in a belly; a black and white flattened triangular view from the ultrasound machine. Then everyone talked about knowing the gender while passing it around. I held it the longest— fascinated by the thumbnails on the right side of the page. One was an ad for winter vacation swim wear, another for a flat tummy diet via work out videos, and finally, Botox surgery. A real ink zap. Over the womb read: I LOVE YOU. I wondered if that's how the file came from the doctor or if the parent went into Photoshop to decorate the fetus.

Dear Photographer:

The performance would have been better if there weren't so many cameras around it. Two tripods set up a barrier between the stage and the audience. I felt like I might knock over the legs of the tripods; they sprawled so wide, like roots in a swamp. "Who are you," I asked the guy behind one camera. He said, "she's my wife," pointing to the performer. It was actually a reenactment of a famous performance involving the possibility of torture. Behind this loose stage was a storefront window so people from the street also watched, but it was the backside of activity, which relied on participation.

Dear Photographer:

A flier posted at the local café read, Lost Camera featuring a product shot followed by the location and time the camera went missing. The owner announced that they just want the memory card. I contemplated the chances the person who found the camera would see the flier and then only give back half. The pushpin made it hang low on the bulletin board like an earring weighing down on its puncture. I ripped the flier off the board. It had been weeks since the camera was lost.

Acknowledgements

Lara Durback of NoNo Press published *Picture Cameras* in 2010, which featured many of the captions that appear in this book. Erin Morrill and Andrew Kenower of Trafficker Press edited and published *The Photographer without a Camera* in 2011, where the brain of this book began to grow.

A version of "Press Conference" was performed in July 2012 with Stephen Boyer and Alex DeCarli as the Photographer's Assistants at The Invisible Dog in Brooklyn. For their support and help with this one night performance, thank you: Shonni Enelow, Josh Hoglund, Kristina Satter, Jess Barbagallo, Christine Shallenberg, Alex DeCarli, Chris Giarmo, Nathan Lemoine and Sunita Prasad. A version of "The Sale" was performed in January 2011 at Small Press Traffic's Poets' Theater in San Francisco. Jacqueline Frost, Ted Rees, Matt Runkle and Cassie Thornton played The Photographer's Assistants.

I am grateful to the following publications and editors where traces of *The Photographer* have appeared: 2015 *Boog City Reader* (Nicole Wallace & David Kirschenbaum), *Troubling the Line: Trans and Genderqueer Poetry and Poetics* (Trace Peterson and TC Tolbert), *Dreamboat* (Alli Warren), *The Volta's Evening Will Come Issue 24* (TC Tolbert), *OMG!* (Brandon Brown), *Ragtag* (Nico Peck) *Try!* (Sara Larsen & David Brazil).

The Nonsite Collective engaged the methodologies of this book in a "Photo Response Workshop" in March of 2011 at SF Camerawork. Courtney Johnson's *T_XT_RT* Show in 2010 at Jenkins Johnson Gallery hosted a performance and installation of the "Dear Photographer" letters where Evan Kennedy and I read as newscasters with the surprising addition of live classical music. Nada Gordon & Cori Copp of the Segue Series and Thom Donovan and Dorothea Lasky of Multifarious Array invited me to read substantial portions of this work in 2012 & 2013 in New York.

Jess Barbagallo, Adrienne Garbini, Amanda Davidson, Stephen Boyer, Evan Kennedy, Erin Morrill, Charity Coleman, Sarah Rupp, thank you, for reading drafts of this book. For inspiration and guidance, thank you Susan Gevirtz, Juliana Spahr, Dodie Bellamy, Truong Tran, Stephen Ratcliffe, Erika Staiti, Samantha Giles, Steve Benson, Vilém Flusser, Susan Sontag, bell hooks, Ariella Azoulay, Rabih Mroué, Holly Blake, Headlands Center for the Arts, Community Thrift and Urban Ore, Ellie & Ira Goldberg, Beth Hayes, Rachel Levitsky, Stacy Szymaszek, Dia Felix, Susanna Troxler and Amber Shigg.

ROOF BOOKS
the best in language since 1976

Recent & Selected Titles

· TOP 40 by Brandon Brown. 138 p. $15.95

· DEAD LETTER by Jocelyn Saidenberg. 98 p. $15.95

· THE MEDEAD by Fiona Templeton. 314 p. $19.95

· LYRIC SEXOLOGY VOL. 1 by Trish Salah. 138 p. $15.95

· INSTANT CLASSIC by erica kaufman 90 p. $14.95

· A MAMMAL OF STYLE by Kit Robinson
& Ted Greenwald. 96 p. $14.95

· VILE LILT by Nada Gordon. 114 p. $14.95

· DEAR ALL by Michael Gottlieb. 94 p. $14.95

· FLOWERING MALL by Brandon Brown. 112 p. $14.95.

· MOTES by Craig Dworkin. 88 p. $14.95

· APOCALYPSO by Evelyn Reilly. 112 p. $14.95

· BOTH POEMS by Anne Tardos. 112 p. $14.95

Roof Books are published by
Segue Foundation
300 Bowery · New York, NY 10012
For a complete list,
please visit roofbooks.com

Roof Books are distributed by
SMALL PRESS DISTRIBUTION
1341 Seventh Street · Berkeley, CA. 94710-1403.
spdbooks.org